Manifesting Princess

Live UP to the Reputation!

APRIL CLINE

Copyright © 2011 April Cline Enterprises, LLC.

April Cline Enterprises, LLC.
Hedgesville, WV

All Worldwide Rights Reserved, Hedgesville, WV

All rights reserved. No part of this book may be reproduced by any mechanical, photographic or electronic process, or in the form of a system, transmitted or otherwise be copied for public or private use. Brief quotations from the book may be used for "fair use", such as for articles and reviews of this book, without prior written permission from the author.

The author of this book does not dispense any medical advice or prescribe the use of any technique as a form of treatment for physical or medical problems without the advice of a doctor or physician. The intent of this book is to offer information to support the reader's emotional and spiritual wellbeing. The author, publisher, and any representatives, assume no responsibility for any actions that the reader chooses to take, whether with themselves or anyone else.

ISBN 978-0-615-55836-3

www.ManifestingPrincess.com

Table of Contents

Table of Contents .... - 3 -

Dedication .... - 6 -

Gratitude .... - 8 -

Foreword by Hemal Radia .... - 12 -

What is a Manifesting Princess? .... - 17 -

Mirror, Mirror on the Wall .... - 21 -

Keys to the Kingdom - Using the Law of Attraction .... - 24 -

Losing Your Glass Slipper .... - 33 -

Slaying the Dragons .... - 39 -

Breaking the Spell .... - 45 -

Castles, Carriages & Kingdoms, Oh My! .... - 50 -

Day Dreams Come True .... - 55 -

Creating Your Happily Ever After .... - 60 -

Live UP to the Reputation! .... - 66 -

Confessions from the Castle .... - 71 -

The Magic Wand of Friendship .... - 75 -

Manifesting Support & Coaching ....- 79 -

Manifesting Assignments ....- 83 -

Create a Vision Board ....- 87 -

Quotes by April Cline ....- 92 -

Quotes & Stories from Friends ....- 98 -

Recommended ....- 110 -

About April Cline ....- 111 -

Dedication

To my Mother, Jane, the Queen of my Life.

I miss you.

1929 - 2011

&

To my sons,

Todd, Daniel and Matt

You're the Light of my Life!

Gratitude

There are so many people to thank, but I run the risk of forgetting someone. Everyone in my life as touched me in some way. People have come into my life for a "reason or a season". Each has touched my heart.

To Barb Hildebrand for her friendship and giving me the nick name of the "Manifesting Princess."

To my good friend, writing mentor and Law of Attraction coach, Helen M. Collins, for her infinite support and proofreading skills!

To Hemal Radia, for writing the Foreword to this book, who inspired me to become a LOA Coach in the first place and continued to guide me with his solid example of what a wonderful *citizen of the world* can do!

To the supportive community of LOA'ers at Manifesting Excellence, for your continued "likes" and cheering me on!

To Esther and Jerry Hicks and Abraham, for their explanation of the Law of Attraction and living a spirit-based life while in this earth school.

To Mark Husson, my favorite astrologer, for his humorous good readings every Tuesday on HayHouseRadio.com

To my many Guests on AprilClineRadio.com for enlightening me as I honed my interview skills to become a better radio host!

To my best friends, Jeni Tutwiler and Dawn Hancock, for always being there for me.

To my Facebook friends, Melissa Clevenger Baker, Deborah Hall, Debbie Saviano, Payson Cooper and Dr. Lisa Love, who reached out to me with great compassion, inspired me and cheered me on!

To Donna Gatti, my angel lady, for her inspiring messages from my angels and her "big sister" mentoring.

To Oprah Winfrey, Louise Hay and Cheryl Richardson for blessing my life with their on-going inspirational lives.

To Marci Shimoff, for her books "Happy for No Reason" and "Love for No Reason" which made it all seem so possible!

To Arielle Ford and Mike Koenigs for their "Everything You Should Know" program about writing and publishing a book. I learned so much from their practical, knowledgeable advice!

To my parents, each who have pass on, Reynolds and Jane; without you, I wouldn't be here. With you I became a better person. To my step-father, Neill; your optimism is forever etched in my heart. To my sister, Becky, for her cheerful disposition in spite of repeated obstacles.

To my Virtual Assistant and Graphic Artist, Michelle Medd, of Administrative Essentials, for creating such ease in my life and beauty on the page.

I am so appreciative of everyone who has been a positive role model and good influence in my life.

A special THANK YOU to you, my readers, for buying this book and sharing it with your friends. I look forward to getting to know you!

Foreword by Hemal Radia

I was honoured when April asked me to write the Foreword to her book "Manifesting Princess – Live UP to the Reputation."

Upon reading my book, "Find You & You Find Everything: The Secrets to the Law of Attraction," she has been a part of my Manifesting Excellence Group Coaching Program and we have interacted about the Law of Attraction and in applying it. She has taken this on, with her own experiences and coaching background, and written this lovely book, tying it in with fairy tale and empowerment.

This book in your hands is oriented towards helping women in raising their self-esteem, setting their standards for what they DO want in their lives, and, as I like to put it, finding the divinity (Goddess!) within themselves.

The book is conversational and easy to read and talks about the Law of Attraction from an energetic point of view. There are many out there talking about the Law of Attraction, including with a lot of hype, though I believe that when it is talked about from an energetic or a vibrational point of view that it best empowers the reader.

This is how I've oriented my teaching of it and how April does so in this book here too.

I know that when April started writing this book, she was very much inspired and wrote it in quick time, most of it within a week. You can feel the inspiration as she converses with you through the book.

As you read this book, allow it to serve you in having conscious awareness of your thoughts and your empowerment. Notice what behaviours or habits of thought you have about your life or yourself. Do you always give yourself a hard time about something? Do you not allow your own needs to be as important? There is no reason why you are not as important as anyone else. As you claim your own power, you have more of that to share with those you love.

Although this book encourages self-reflection, it is not about looking back and only doing that. Your power is in your now. What are you choosing to do with your life right now, and where would you like it to go?

My view is as you claim your power, you empower those around you. Not necessarily in an outward aggressive vocal way, but more-so through your inner power. The outer will come as a natural expression of that. You may not even need to say anything. Let the Universe do its work on an energetic level. It's not about how loud you shout that the Universe hears, it's about the clarity in your energy. When you are truly at peace and in alignment with yourself, you won't need to say anything, you'll be too busy doing and being, and things will be happening.

You may ask yourself how you can tap into this power when you have so many responsibilities and commitments. Allow yourself to create a little bit of time and space for yourself. Does that feel better? If it does, continue. Sometimes we make ourselves busy and we do not get to hear ourselves and our intuition. Start to follow your inner voice. Many "responsibilities and commitments" come from habits and perceptions that we have created. Allow yourself some inner space, and see what opens up. As you find strength in that, you may find that some things are not as important to you as they used to be, other things open up, and you have a strength within you, energetically, for whatever it is you *do* choose to do.

As you do this and you "find yourself", you will be changing the energy within you. As you do that you will be drawing different aspects from others and from the world around you and it will act as a confirmation of the energy shifts you have made. Do not be surprised if sometimes there is early 'turbulence' when you go through changes in finding yourself from one place to another, energetically. Look at this as an opportunity you are being given regarding the choices you are making. A wonderful opportunity to be aware of the perspectives of the choices you are making. It will enable you to have clarity about what *is* important to you. This is something you will know for yourself.

Settle back, enjoy the 'fairy tale', and the bringing to life of your own story, and we look forward to hearing about it and your journey.

Hemal Radia

Author of "*Find You & You Find Everything: The Secrets to the Law of Attraction*", 'Super' Coach, and Speaker. www.HemalRadia.com

What is a Manifesting Princess?

Once upon a time, I believed in fairy tales and pleasing others. Just like my favorite heroine, Cinderella, I had the good girl syndrome down to perfection and I took care of everyone's needs, waiting patiently for my turn to receive acts of kindness and love. I waited for my Prince Charming to come along. Fast forward two husbands and three children later and I am alone, in my fifties and starting over.

So, what is a Manifesting Princess? She is a woman who knows who she is and what she wants. She learns everything she can about herself and moves forward in her life with her head held high and her self worth held even higher.

But how do you get to that point? It's the journey, actually. Living up to the reputation of being a Manifesting Princess is a decision. I decided to try to live UP to the reputation of being a Manifesting Princess, and what I received in return, was a jaw dropping, eye opening, spell binding, roller coaster ride.

In my roller coaster ride, I mean "journey", I discovered that the higher I held myself in high esteem, the greater the challenges and the greater the rewards.

When I thought better of myself, thought about what I deserved, what I should and shouldn't live with (or without), when I stood my ground, when I spoke my truth, I found out that I was not alone, that I was loved, that I was liked, and I received greater respect.

It was a domino effect. The more I thought good things, the more good things and people, came into my life.

You know the law of attraction and what you think about expands, you create your own reality, and all that stuff from "The Secret"? *Well, it turns out its true!*

Try this… think of something really sad, hurtful or angry; notice how you feel. Now think about the happiest time in your life. Feel the difference? That's energy. That's the POWER of your thoughts!

Just imagine if you were to think those good thoughts more often, you would feel better more often. If you felt better more often, what kind of life would you have? Can you even begin to imagine the kind of people, money, business, excitement, adventure, fun you'd attract into your life?

Answer this question: What would you do if you knew you couldn't fail?

A Manifesting Princess is a woman who thinks the good thoughts and grows from each little step she takes toward manifesting her own excellence, and is rewarded with a higher vibration in her energy, which attracts other people with higher energy (like goes with like).

She is a Princess at making her dreams into a reality and knows that everything she thinks and does today will be what she reaps tomorrow.

Your thoughts will give you the "Keys to the Kingdom" and allow you to live your wildest, most desirable dreams, simply by raising your vibrational energy by changing how you think and what you focus on.

Sounds easy? Sounds hard? The answer is YES to both. It is easy and it is hard.

However, if you're sick and tired of cleaning up after your "ugly step sisters" and want to go to the "Fancy Dress Ball" and become the Princess who is lavished on and loved and has this beautiful, whirlwind, royal life – then you have to do your homework!

So, grab your Tiara and let's get started!

Mirror, Mirror on the Wall

There was a time when being the "fairest of them all" was all it took to succeed in life, and there was a time when I was the fairest of them all. I took great pride in my looks and how I dressed and had a beautiful figure, home, husband, children, dinner parties, and Christmas photos – the works! I was Suzy Homemaker and Linda Lovelace all rolled into one fantastical stay at home Mom.

Unfortunately, looks fade, I got a little thicker in the middle than I'd planned, and my children grew up, got married and moved away, leaving me with Prince Charming, and his interest in everything except me.

If you've never focused on yourself before, then you're going to have a bit of a bumpy ride. You have to know yourself and who you are in order to even know what to dream about, wish for, and manifest.

One of the questions that I used to dread answering was, *"Tell me about yourself."* I never knew what to say. I was a housewife with a husband and children. I was on the PTA Board, went to Church every Sunday and had friends and family over for every holiday. I was plenty busy. I didn't have time to know myself.

So, I'll ask you... *tell me about yourself.* Do you like yourself? Do you like your life? Do you think you're pretty? Are you proud of your accomplishments? Do you think you're someone special? Are you worth knowing?

Mirror, mirror on the Wall... she doesn't like herself at all!

Does that about sum it up?

My dear Manifesting Princess, what you put in front of the mirror is a direct reflection, literally, of how you feel about yourself. So, if you have been hiding things – guess what? You've been found out just by having the extra weight on your hips, the circles under your eyes, the dry hair, and the dull skin, the frown on your face, the frumpy clothes and the fatigue you drag around every day. It just screams "*I don't like myself*!"... Even though you say you're "fine" when someone asks you how you're doing. No you're not, and everyone knows. Everyone, except you.

Don't worry, all is not lost! There is hope! There is joy and happiness for you. And, yes, even sleeping through the night, I promise!

Follow me! Together we will get you the *Keys to the Kingdom*!

Keys to the Kingdom - Using the Law of Attraction

I magine a big funnel. At the bottom is the tip, the beginning of the "V". At the top is the wide open top of the funnel.

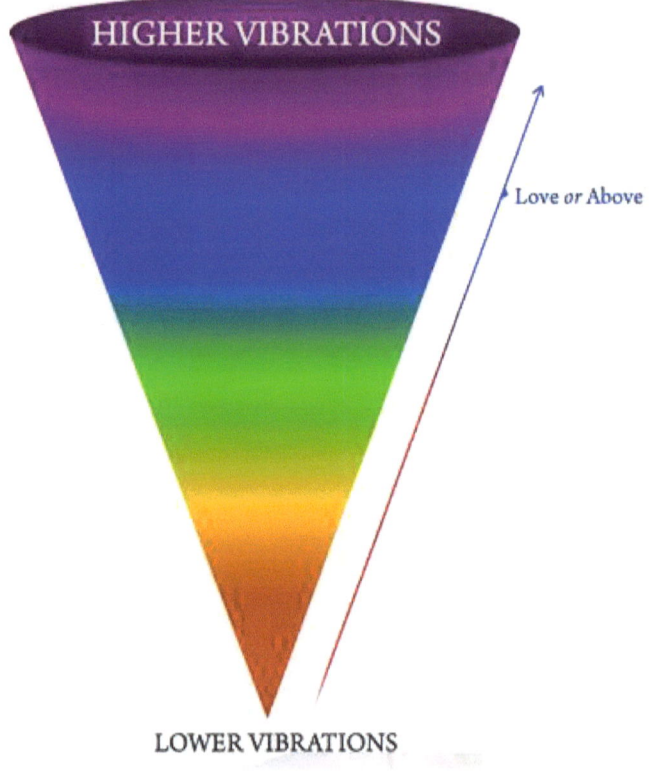

*www.loveorabove.com

This funnel represents your vibrational energy; the lower the energy, the lower the frequency of your vibration – your energy. Since everything is energy, you will only attract the same energy level to you. Just like if you put your television on channel 7 but wish, hope, pray for channel 22, you won't get channel 22... you'll get channel 7 because you're sending out channel 7 energy.

Let's discuss some examples of vibrational energy. You'll be spellbound!

Examples of lower vibration:

- Gossiping
- Arguing
- Swearing
- Negative talk of any kind
- Envy, jealousy, being unkind
- Fearful and misleading reporting
- Tragic stories
- Poverty
- Abuse or abusing substance
- Reading, listening or watching anything that encourages any of the above.

- Disrespecting yourself by overeating, not taking time for sleep, exercise, good hygiene, chaotic environment, being in debt, even a purse that's over flowing can be a sign that you don't think highly of yourself!

Ways to raise your vibration:
- Smile
- Laugh
- Prayer
- Daydream
- Speak with respect
- Speak affirmations
- Give a compliment
- Write something nice to yourself or someone
- Eat good food
- Fresh Flowers or plants
- Raw Chocolate
- Window shopping so you can day dream
- Listen or read or watch self-development and law of attraction
- Enjoying the company of friendly, happy people
- Listening to good music

- Dancing
- Acts of service
- Paying your bills – staying in a budget
- Being your authentic self

Maybe I should put this another way. You're shopping at Kmart but you really want to shop at Saks Fifth Avenue. Chances are Saks is in a completely separate part of town. You're going to have to look the part before you even go into Saks as well, so you'll have to go home and change into your nicest outfit, best jewelry, and then go back to the car and drive to Saks.

When you walk in to Saks Fifth Avenue, it's serene, it's quiet, and there aren't many people there, because everything is so expensive. You're greeted and waited on for your every need. They'll even do a fashion show for you and give you a personal shopper!

There's no stepping over cigarette butts, as you walk from your car in the parking lot, to the store front, no crashing of shopping carts, no blue light specials, babies crying, or long lines to stand in.

Which store would you rather shop at? How does it make you feel? Notice that feeling. It's critical to notice and to get to know that feeling because it will be your guide throughout the rest of your life in your journey to being a Manifesting Princess and obtaining the *Keys to the Kingdom* – it's the Law of Attraction at work!

How do you attract that royal treatment into your real life? The Saks Fifth Avenue attitude on a Kmart budget? Notice how you feel right now just thinking about the difference. Take that same feeling with you, wherever you shop, and you will begin to attract at a higher vibrational energy level. It might be smaller things at first, like a great parking space, a short line at the grocery store at 5:00 p.m., or unexpected money appearing in your bank account. Watch for it. It will happen.

Stay away from lower vibration. If you must be in a lower vibration area or with a person with lower vibration, then close your eyes as often as you can and daydream/dream/think about something that you really want. Maybe it's a boyfriend, a bouquet of fresh flowers, a new computer, a new car, whiter teeth, to be rid of those extra 25 pounds.

Imagine, dream and think about what you really want, what you wish will come true. Dream about it, write about it, and you will raise your vibration simply by thinking about it – yes even if you're at a job you hate!

A Dream is a Wish Your Heart Makes.
~ Cinderella

    This is where Vision Boards can be so helpful. Tear out photos, words, etc., from magazines and paste them into a spiral bound artist book – or even a simple school notebook that your kid isn't using anymore. Handwrite your dreams and desires on the pages. Fill them up and look at the "vision" as often as you possibly can, but especially before you go to bed.

    When you go to bed, decide what you're going to dream about. I began doing this when I was a little girl. I used to have favorite stories to keep me occupied until I fell asleep. I still do it to this day.

    Another thing I did is I found a great photo of a couple in love and it's been my screen saver on my computer, for about three years now. This instantly raises my vibration!

    Climbing further up the funnel, you can raise your vibration by singing, dancing, humming a tune, reading a poem, laughing, holding a baby, petting your dog or cat, lighting a candle, inhaling a fragrance you like, applying essential oils or diffusing them in your home, dressing nicely, getting a good haircut, going for a walk in nature, meditating, getting a massage or other energy work – any of these will raise your vibration.

Here's a quick and easy way to raise your vibration no matter what, even if you don't feel like it – in fact, especially if you don't feel like it… SMILE. You just have to turn up the corners of your mouth and you will release happy chemicals throughout your body! Isn't that amazing?

You're almost to the top of the wide open funnel…

The best way to raise your vibrational energy is to surround yourself with positive people who already have a higher vibration. You can do this by starting a law of attraction book club, participating in an online group, hiring a Law of Attraction coach, attending group or private calls about positive things, and go to movies with your friends that will make you laugh (the friends and the movies). No friends? Then go alone, laugh yourself silly and I guarantee you will begin attracting people to you like a magnet!

Serving others is also an excellent way to raise your vibration and also give back. It tells the Universe that you're grateful, that you feel the abundance in your life so much that you're willing to take the time to spend time with others who need someone to visit with them, or to help them in some way.

Remember that Random Acts of Kindness are great for zooming up your energetic flow super quickly! If you're really down in the dumps or having a lot of "negative" low energy things happening in your life, go out and give unto others! You will stop the lower vibrations in their tracks, do a complete 180 and begin magnetically attracting good things into your life again. You reap what you sow; it's all part of the golden rule, no matter what your religious background!

Keep this up and you'll have the Keys to the Kingdom!

Can't you just hear the jingle of those keys now?

Losing Your Glass Slipper

Along the way to making changes in our life, we all slip up and lose our way. Getting back on track can be easier than you think!

After losing my glass slipper, I fell into a deep depression – maybe the evil witch cast a spell on me, but it felt like depression! I slept all day, didn't eat, or ate the wrong food. Isolating myself was something I was good at. I wouldn't even go the grocery store, except at night, about 30 minutes before they closed, just so I wouldn't run into anyone!

It's sort of like falling down the rabbit hole…

One day, while taking a nap, I had a terrible dream that I was dying and was afraid that no one would ever know that I had died. I'd long since given up my friends. I'd pushed them all away. I stopped going to any activities. I didn't even bother to answer my phone. No one knew I existed. No one would miss me.

I woke up completely terrified! This wasn't a dream, it was a premonition, or the kick in the pants that I needed desperately! I texted a friend and asked her what time our monthly brunch was for the next day, and I got up and forced myself to go to brunch with these friends that hadn't seen me in months.

Being around people, especially people you like and who like you, raises your vibrational energy immediately. Suddenly you're smiling again, even if it's just to be polite. You're all dressed up, you're sitting in a restaurant and you begin to remember that book you want to write and the way you want to live the rest of your life.

Get out a notebook and map out a blueprint for your life. Scribble it on the wall if you have to but get clear on what you want to do with your life. Then set your INTENTION about how you're going to accomplish these things.

If you do this, it will stop the negativity immediately and you will begin to flourish, and then guess what…You're attracting other like-minded individuals into your energy field and you're thinking life is good again! Life is good! You can even sing it or write it or just chatter away about how wonderful life is – *because what you think about you bring about.* What you put your mind on will expand!

You literally create your reality.

Now, stand next to a mirror hanging on the wall. You can see what is reflected in that mirror, can't you?

That mirror is reflecting what its reality is. It really shows what it sees… The furniture, the candy dish, the keys on the table, whatever is in the mirror is there because someone placed it within the scope of the mirror.

The same is true with your life, with your reality…. If there is a bully abusing you or demeaning you - yes, that's right – you put that person in your life, because as Dr. Phil says *"We teach people how to treat us."*

Any self-respecting Manifesting Princess would **never** tolerate abuse of any kind. No yelling, no swearing, no emotional, verbal or physical violence to herself or her loved ones!

A Manifesting Princess is NOT codependent! So, if you are living a lie, living with a liar, living with a bully, allowing yourself to be bullied – then you get yourself out of that relationship immediately. But you have to ask yourself, what part of you is a bully to have attracted a bully? What part of you is a liar to have attracted a liar? What part of you is a cheater, to have attracted a cheater?

Maybe it's because you think you don't deserve any better. Maybe it's because this is the way your parents were and how you were raised. That men disrespected women and women just had to "take it".

Now, that's enough to make anyone cry, but especially this Manifesting Princess *because I have been there and know your pain.* Maybe you feel that I have led a storybook 'charmed' life…. Not so! This Manifesting Princess has learned everything the hard way and I want to lift you up, but you have to be willing to take the first step.

Love yourself enough to live a peaceful, happy life, because you deserve peace. Give yourself, and your children, that gift of a drama free life, because no wants the police and the court system in their private business. You deserve a life where you are loved, so become and speak loving. You deserve the peace of soft, respectful speaking, not yelling or shouting. Speak softly, speak with respect, and you will have that reflected back to you.

Be that person. Become that person. How? By attracting what you want in life instead of what you have now. Take a stand.

There is an old saying, *"Stand for something or you'll fall for anything."*

On the other hand, maybe your victim story is just too important to you. Hanging onto that victim story allows you to receive the low vibration of pity, but the focus remains on you, so maybe you think it's worth it. It's not. Besides, your children deserve better, so do it for them. Get yourself out of bad relationships; remove yourself from poverty as quickly as you can. Get an education. Improve your poor health, chronic pain, and a host of bad choices. Sober up, literally, and become the Manifesting Princess you were born to be.

It's okay to lose your way, but it's not okay to stay there.

Now that you have the keys to leave the dungeon, make a run for the drawbridge and into the Castle where dreams really do come true!

Slaying the Dragons

Every Heroine has her "Dragons". Cinderella had her step-mother. Sleeping Beauty pricked her finger. Rapunzel was kept in a tower and you have your negative thoughts. Don't underestimate a negative thought. It can lead to all kinds of calamity!

You can't afford the luxury of a negative thought!

Into every life a little rain must fall, there must be opposition in all things, nothing in life is easy, but, when it comes to dealing with negativity, you have really got to watch yourself. It has been said that by the time you speak the negative thought, you have thought it approximately 300 times. That is a lot of negativity.

What negativity will do is lower your vibration and bring you MORE negativity. If you complain about it, you'll get even MORE to complain about! So, it's the stubbed toe theory – you wake up in the morning and you stub your toe. You're jumping up and down, holding your foot yelling "OUCH!" and it seems like the whole day is not set to spiral downward.

The same is true with the Dragon called negativity. You say one negative word, and the whole paragraph comes out.

It's like eating potato chips… you can't have just one, you have to have the whole bag!

Next thing you know you're whining and complaining, bickering and then arguing with people. You stomp off. You're angry because "nothing ever works out for me" and you slam the door to your room and pout! You'll show 'em! You stuff your face with chocolate you've hidden in your room, call a friend who will listen to you complain, giving the negative low energy even more energy – the Universe says, "O*kay you want more to complain about…you've got it!*" and you get MORE problems than you know how to handle. Your transmission falls out, right after you're pulled over for not seeing the red light you just ran through. You call the tow truck and find out it will be $75 just to tow it and $150 for your ticket. Your balance is zero in the bank, so you've got to go to your parents and ask them to bail you out – again! You are up to your eyeballs in debt and the collection companies are now calling you. You feel like you're drowning and then your boyfriend breaks up with you as he's driving you home and now you have no way to get to work in the morning.

Now you're putting the last nail in when you say, "What else can go wrong?" (Note: don't ever say that!) The door to your apartment has a pink sign on it with an eviction notice, the locks have been changed and your neighbor has all your stuff.

Just STOP! Stop and take a breath. Sit down. Close your eyes. Focus on your breathing. Take long slow breaths. Drink some water and if you know EFT (Emotional Freedom Technique) do some tapping. If not, then just stop everything and sit and be quiet.

What has happened is you are getting a message from the Universe. The message is to slow down and get your act together.

How do you get your act together? By taking full responsibility for everything you think, say, and do. No excuses! Everything! Every thought. Every action. Every Reaction. They are your choices. Own them. No more victim stories about poor little you. Didn't you watch Cinderella? Well, she had a Fairy Godmother come rescue her. You have yourself!

There are No Victims, only Volunteers!

If you ever needed to know yourself, this is the moment! If you ever needed to learn to *Slay your own Dragons,* this is the moment! If you're ever going to take a stand or fall for anything, now is the time!

Stand in front of a mirror and say the following: *I love life and life loves me. (Louise Hay). Life Loves Me. Life Loves Me. (say it again) LIFE LOVES ME! Now take out your cell phone and text yourself – LIFE LOVES ME and post it on your Facebook wall, tweet it and go back to the mirror and write it in lipstick across the mirror.*

LIFE LOVES ME. ~ Louise Hay

I want you to do this for ten minutes four times a day. Every day and then watch what happens. You will immediately begin to feel better. You will begin to look for ways that life loves you. You will find ways that life loves you and you will have slayed that Dragon yourself in the process! You are a beautiful, triumphant, Manifesting Princess, and *I'm so proud of you!*

Step into the center of the stage, the spotlight is on you… take a bow, pat yourself on the back, jump for joy and applaud yourself for standing up and loving life. In the process, you have raised your vibrational energy 100 fold and will immediately begin attracting higher frequencies to your energy field. The phone will ring and it will be about a raise or taking a day off with pay. You'll receive a gift in the mail; you'll stand taller, expect better and receive a better life in the process.

You will reap what you sow. You will get back what you have given. And, *my* Beatle, Sir Paul McCartney says this: *"The Love you get is equal to the Love you give."* Give love and receive love. Give without expectation of anything in return and raise your vibration even higher!

The Dragon has been slayed by you, my dear! Keep your self-esteem high and your self worth even higher and the Dragon wouldn't dare bother you anymore!

Breaking the Spell

We all have days where everything seems to be going wrong. Nothing is working. Everything you touch explodes, spills, goes hay wire. You can't get anything to work right. You have no patience, you're yelling at people, you can't focus… you're just not yourself! Everything seems to wrong and like you're under a "Spell".

I had one of those days just before I finished writing this book. I was falling apart at the seams one day. I spilled my protein drink all over my brand new yellow top, my phone wouldn't work, neither would my computer, I ended up going to bed and crying. I'd been sick the weekend before…what I really needed was some more rest! After napping, I realized what I really needed was a good cry on a friend's shoulder, so I put out an SOS to a group of friends and my phone began to ring off the hook!

I was careful NOT to complain too much and I chose my words very carefully, because I didn't want more of the same coming after me. I didn't want to attract more bad days. I'm very happy to be able to tell you my personal recipe for "Breaking the Spell".

Ending the struggle is the key to breaking the spell. You have to acknowledge that there is something going on, without giving too much energy to it, lest you end up attracting more of it to you!

First of all, if you're not feeling well, go back to bed and try to get some sleep. Sometimes, things don't go well because we really need some rest. So go and take that break from life and just sleep or rest away your cares!

Put on some music and dance around the house and/or go outside for a walk. Being in nature, or just outside of your house will magically change your attitude no matter what the weather!

Phone a friend. Actually pick up the phone and call a friend! Tell them you need to talk, but only take half the time so that they can talk, too! If that isn't enough, then call another friend!

I've found that talking to someone helps me to get out of my own stuff and think about someone else for a change. And change is the key word here!

Next, get out your journal or log on to your blog and start writing! Write about the challenges, the feelings that are bubbling up. You will have an opportunity to read it all later… just keep writing! Get your anger, unhappiness, depress out by writing it all down! You can even wad it up and throw it away when you're done!

By now you should be feeling a lot better. Take a deep breath and let it out slowly! Ahhhhhhhhh!!

The Spell is Broken!

By intending – as you are moving into a segment of relationships – to focus upon your points of harmony; to give your great attention, not to what you are disagreeing about, but to the things you agree upon...that is the resolution in all relationships. For when you focus on what you do not like, by the Law of Attraction, you solicit more of what you do not want.

~ Abraham-Hicks

What I noticed the next morning is that I wasn't as lonely during the day because of the level of interaction I'd had the day, evening and night before! It completely surprised me, but it makes sense. By having someone over for coffee, or eating dinner with someone, going shopping, going for a walk, chatting on the phone, it all sent my vibrational energy zooming up and my frequency is now elevated, even the next day. So today has already gone better and I have a date for lunch later this week.

I know that sometimes these "rules" can seem complicated, but they are truly so simple. Live today the way you want tomorrow to be.

Let me put this another way. *If you want tomorrow to be happy, then be happy today!*

I keep going back to the basics that you reap what you sow. Plant the bulbs in October for beautiful flowers in the Spring.

The same way we exercise and diet so much. We want to look better than we look now. That's the Law of Attraction at work, too!

When you're planning a big event, like perhaps your wedding, you day dream, you make lists, you meet with your wedding planner, you schedule time to go shopping, you choose all the right things for the upcoming event. Isn't that the same as "what you sow so shall ye reap"?

Spend time day dreaming to become the magnetic attractor of your dreams and they will undeniably come to you because it is law! Stay within that vibration for as long as you can. The longer you hold onto that frequency, the sooner that which you are attracting, will come to you.

Congratulations, you've broken the spell!

Castles, Carriages & Kingdoms, Oh My!

I magine a world where everything you want is available to you; where your every want is fulfilled, your every need anticipated and met. Every thirst is quenched. You haven't a care in the world. Every Dream comes true!

This world exists already and is waiting for you to inhabit it. This world is in your imagination, in your thoughts and in your dreams. It can become a reality if you really want it. It is yours for the taking.

Receive the world for which it is, not what it's not.
~ Unknown

I invite you to create beauty wherever you go. Create a beautiful home for yourself – even if you're sleeping on a friends' couch, make it as lovely as possible – clean sheets, scented with lavender, fluffy pillows, cozy blanket and you're all set.

At work, or school or wherever you're at, leave the place better than you found it. Pick up trash, wipe the counter, put things away, and tidy up. Let people know that having a clean, organized, beautiful environment is important to you and watch the level of respect, and your vibrational energy rise.

Dress immaculately. Your grooming should be worthy of a Princess! How can you manifest when you're a mess? Clean up, fix up and straighten up and you will *Live UP to the Reputation of the Manifesting Princess!*

When you have everything at your disposal, and you do, then you'll want to take advantage of that and take a bite out of life to fully enjoy it. I'm sure you will have many "ladies in waiting" to go have lunch with and all the charming Princes will be lining up when they see how you carry yourself with such high esteem. You'll be able to have the life of your dreams, but you'll be able to love it and enjoy every moment, because you are grateful!

Gratitude changes everything and raises your vibrational energy exponentially!

I'm sure you've heard that Oprah has kept a Gratitude journal and swears it has changed her life. So I challenge you to do the same. Keep a Gratitude journal. Write down everything you have to be grateful for, all the abundance in your life, the many blessings and lucky stars you've been endowed with. Give thanks for anything and everything. I run around my house saying "Thank You" several times a day… for no specific reason… I just say "Thank You!" to the Universe, my Angels, my ancestors, and everyone on the other side who is helping me with my life. Thank you Thank you Thank you!

When you are in a grateful state of mind, you will not be tempted to be negative. You won't be the least bit tempted to complain, and you won't even think about watching FOX news or Entertainment Tonight or the Fashion Police, because they're dripping with caustic commentary that will lead you straight down to the *Dragon's lair*!

Remaining in a state of Gratitude will ramp up your vibration, your frequency will be incredible and you'll attract so much goodness to you that you really will not be able to contain it!

Write down five things you're grateful for, right now… you'll be so grateful that you did!

I can create Castles as easily as buttons! When you understand the Laws, then you understand that it is not more difficult to create a castle than it is a button. They are equal. It is not more difficult to create $10 million than $100,000. It is the same application of the same Law to two different intentions.

~ Abraham-Hicks

Day Dreams Come True

Disney wrote "A Dream is a wish your heart makes" or was that Cinderella? Same thing, right?

Well, a dream really is a wish your heart makes. A dream is something you wish will come true and if you do it right, it is my opinion, that dreams really can come true.

The Law of Attraction teaches us that what we think about EXPANDS. So if you think about something enough, it will happen. Try it. For the next week say "*I keep getting checks in the mail!*" Say it over and over. Tell all your friends and family. Say it like it's the craziest thing, but gee it just keeps happening!

Wait a week or two… and then, I bet you have checks in the mail!

I believe this so much that I have been proclaiming the art of day dreaming as a tool to manifest your dreams. From big dreams to small dreams, and everything in between, dreams can come true if you focus on them. You can't just sit around and dream, you have to take some action, but day dreaming really is a powerful tool to ATTRACT what you want into your life.

For example, graphics for this book seemed to elude me. For two months I had graphics sent to me by various artists, but nothing was resonating with me; they just weren't right!

Finally, I was close to publishing and really needed my book cover to be done. I needed a graphic designer to quickly create my book cover so I could go to press! This was urgent! So, I took a hint from my own book and I laid down on my couch and day dreamed.

I visualized the cover of my book, the colors, the graphics, the words, the details. Oh it was beautiful (and it is!) I could literally see it in my mind. So I opened my eyes and began to talk to my ceiling fan about this incredible book cover and this wonderful graphic artist that I'd met on Facebook. How talented she is, how efficient and creative and professional! I described in finite detail, in present tense, how nice it was to HAVE this book cover done and now I was off to get the website finished and the graphics for that, etc.

By the time I was done day dreaming, 20 minutes had gone by, but I felt like this "burden" of finding someone to make my book cover, was off my shoulders, that it was done and taken care of; I no longer had to worry about it and I put it in the past!

The key is speaking in the PRESENT and PAST TENSE, as if it were already true!

I logged onto Facebook, without even thinking about my Day Dreaming Method™ session, and met my graphic artist, had a phone call with her later that evening, and she began work the next day!

Wouldn't you agree that the book cover came out really fantastic? I love it! My dream really came true because of my Day Dreaming Method™ session, where I saw my dream completed and taken care of.

Now it's your turn. What is your heart's desire? What dream are you wishing? Maybe you haven't even told yourself because it seemed silly or unrealistic. It's really not! You can have anything you dream of if you want it badly enough!

Just try this. Lie down in a comfortable position, close your eyes and start to visualize your dream. Imagine what it would feel like to be there. What are some of the sights, sounds and smells? What does it feel like? What are you wearing? What are you doing? Imagine that you are in that dream doing exactly what you've dreamed of doing. Now hold that feeling and just stay in that day dream feeling for as long as you can. That is the feeling that will ATTRACT the dream to you like a MAGNET!

Abraham-Hicks says, *"Your thoughts are powerful, attractive magnets – attracting one to another. Thoughts attract to themselves, and you attract thoughts to you by giving your attention to them. Those who speak most of prosperity have it, and those who speak most of sickness or poverty have it. It is Law. It can be no other way."*

Right now, as you are day dreaming, the magnet is literally pulling that dream directly to you! Your energy field is sending out a vibrational frequency that the Universe must obey! It will send like to like. Whatever you're attracting, will be attracted to you!

If it's a guy, or a job, or money, or a hobby, a form of recognition, maybe winning something – day dream about it, because it will come true if you continue to hold that day dream feeling frequently throughout the day, every day, until it comes true!

You create your reality and your dreams can become your reality if you do your day dreaming sessions and also make sure you place yourself in the position of being able to receive this dream. You can't just sit at home and wish. You have to go out and go after it, but if you add them together, you're going to succeed because of the Universal Law of Attraction!

Keep Day Dreaming!

Creating Your Happily Ever After

Happiness is a choice. It is also a state of mind. It requires great, mindful discipline to choose to be happy. Each of us has our own struggles to overcome, but we always have a choice of how we're going to react to them.

> *No matter how your heart is grieving, if you keep on believing, the dreams that you wish, will come true!*
> *~ Cinderella*

Someone recently asked me if praying would be perceived as lack of faith in the law of attraction. My answer was a profound "No." I firmly believe the prayer raises our vibrational frequency to one of the highest levels. So does meditation and sitting quietly and sending good thoughts to someone. The law of attraction does not replace these options. It is a Universal law that you can use to your advantage.

If you hold your keys up and release them, they will fall to the ground. That's the law of gravity. If you give, you will receive. That's the law of abundance. If you express gratitude for what you have, you have more to be grateful for. It's like that hymn "Count Your Blessings, Name them One by One." When you focus on what you have, you have more to focus on.

The same is true about lack. If you focus on the loss and the things wrong in your life, what you're lacking, watch how quickly you have more lack.

I used to get so frustrated with my friend, Sherry, because she would never complete a sentence that was negative or complaining or if she was feeling frustrated or worried about something. It drove me crazy! I kept saying that the Universe could take it! Go on and just say it. Astrologer, Mark Husson, also says that he doesn't believe that we have to censor the words that we speak for fear of repercussion from the Universe.

When I had the chance, I whined and complained about everything to anyone who would listen. Oh poor me! My victim story was so important to me! How I'd been wronged and how this person hurt me and that person did this, and I was just so invested in being the injured party.

The Universe delivered one bad thing after another because that's what I attracted to myself! Like goes with like, remember?

The silence was deafening and defining.

One day I was lying on my bed and looked over at this beautiful round mirror that belonged to my Grandfather. It is over a desk that I use as a vanity to put my make-up on, so the mirror hangs pretty low. So, I am looking at what is IN this mirror…I could see the walls, the photos on the walls, the floor lamp, the door to the bathroom, the back of the make-up mirror, the Kleenex, the books, the candles and the tops of the pillows on my bed. It dawned on me that this is what the Universe does… this is what the law of attraction does, it reflects back to you precisely and exactly what you put in it. I put those things "in" the mirror. I did it. They wouldn't have been there if I hadn't put them there. So, I literally created that image, that reflection.

If it's true about the mirror then it has to be true about what I place in my life, too. It was a major epiphany for me!

I create my reality – it's really true!

From that moment on I began to look at things differently. Do I really want to watch that TV show and place all that drama and negativity into my brain? Do I really want to dress like this? Do I really want to eat like this? Do I really want to spend money like this? What do I want to manifest with the choices I make?

Things were really changing quickly. Everything is energy, so whatever my energetic field is sending out is exactly what I will get back! Wow, I really got it that time!

Yikes, I'm attracting what my vibrational energy frequency likes. Like a magnet, I am pulling the same to me that I am. Amazing isn't it?

So, creating my own "happily ever after" became my goal. In what way did I want happiness to manifest in my life? How did I want happiness to show up for me?

I began to indulge in something I love to do…daydream! Mmmm, daydreaming is fantastic! You can have, be, do anything you want. Just last night I imagined that I was the one marrying Paul McCartney….again (it's a recurring dream). You can daydream about anyone and anything you'd like to have happen in your life.

When you day dream your vibration zooms way up. It's like you're imagining that this has really happened. So, what I did was I spent time speaking about my new love in the present and past tense, how we met, how we spend our time, what we like about each other, where we go and things we do together.

For me, it has been life changing because I feel myself sending out wondrous waves of energy that will draw him to me, eventually, when I'm ready.

To live our "happily ever after", regardless of what is happening in our lives requires letting go of our victim story, realizing that life is short. Don't waste your time doing things that will bring you down. Do the things that will make your heart sing! Be happy now!

It is a choice to be happy. What will you choose?

Live UP to the Reputation!

Living UP to the reputation of being a Manifesting Princess is a conscious choice. You might want to think about how a Princess would live, dress, conduct her life. If you really are worthy of all the goodness that life has to offer, then place that tiara on your head and become the light to the world you were meant to be!

Act and think and be the Manifesting Princess by acting, thinking and behaving like one. An open mind, less judgment, no gossiping, no behavioral issues, an even temperament, nicely dressed, better posture, a balanced checkbook and even a clean & organized purse!

Most of all a Manifesting Princess speaks in the present tense as if she has already manifesting that which she desires. She speaks that she already possesses the serenity and bliss she's been looking for. She already has the great relationships she's always wanted. She enjoys the riches of the money she has and if she has to speak about something negative, she says "in the past, I used to…" so as to not affirm that negativity in the present time.

A Manifesting Princess has an attitude of confidence, not only in the Universe, but in herself, as she has learned to lean on herself and to include people who match her energetic flow into her life. She surrounds herself with goodness and things that are good for her, because she knows that what she does today is what she will receive tomorrow.

There is a certain peace that comes from ending the struggle, and going with the flow, the energetic flow of life and the Universal Law of Attraction.

Like begets like. If you think about something, it will expand and be in your life very soon – so be careful what you think about!

Confidence is one of the best rewards for ending the struggle. You will learn that you can overcome any obstacle, endure any problem and rise above any assault, simply by being your truest self and believing that you can endure all things.

You are enough.

Doesn't that statement above take some pressure off you? Knowing that you're enough, that you don't have to prove anything to anyone that you don't have to fight and compete for every bit of attention or reward. You really are enough, just because you're here.

Simply stepping into your role as a Manifesting Princess, will allow you to release the constraints of the world and you'll spread your wings and soar high above the petty things and you'll take the proverbial road less traveled.

Bliss will be the rule, and not the exception. Living UP to the reputation of being a Manifesting Princess will be easy. You'll feel the burdens lifted off your shoulders. You'll step more confidently in the world, you'll dress and conduct yourself in a way that you're happy with so that at the end of the day you are pleased. You no longer worry about pleasing other people. Instead you don't worry at all!

Energetically your vibrational frequency is so attractive that you will be sought after by many, simply because they want to know what your "secret" is. And the best part is that you can tell them, if they're ready to listen!

I must warn you that being a beacon of light, you will draw people to you and be given exceptional opportunities to live up to the reputation. There will be people who will seek to destroy you and your reputation. You will tick some people off because some people are not happy unless you're unhappy.

Be happy and continue moving forward as you light the world.

If you've hurt someone's feelings, always offer some kind of solace or ask forgiveness, however, do not allow yourself to be manipulated by their issues.

I have noticed that the higher I climb after my dreams, the more challenging situations I find myself in. I want to reach out and make sure everyone likes me, but that's simply not possible or healthy.

Walk your talk. Rise to the occasion and continue on your journey to Live Up to the Reputation of being a Manifesting Princess!

Confessions from the Castle

Just when you think it's safe to cross the drawbridge, you fall into the moat and nearly drown.

It turns out that living up to the reputation of being a Manifesting Princess, isn't as easy as it sounds. There are stumbling blocks along the cobblestone streets leading to the Kingdom.

Maybe you're still cursed with a "Cinderella Complex" and feel the need to hang on to your "Prince Charming" even when he is behaving more like the frogs you've kissed along the way.

Perhaps you're in love with being a "Damsel in Distress" and like being rescued by the Knight on the white horse. You create circumstances and drama in your life to bring you down, so that "he" can pick you up.

You've been told that you can't do "it", or you don't want to live in the Castle alone. You're tired of going to the "Drancy Fess Balls" and speed dating all the men in the Kingdom. You've tried on endless pairs of glass slippers, and none of them fit.

You're exhausted and you just want your very own Prince Charming!

Well, join the club. Don't we all!

There are many books written about finding Prince Charming and yet most of us will spend the last third of our lives alone. Maybe it's time we all learned to love ourselves and learn that being alone doesn't mean we're lonely, but sometimes we are lonely for that companion we'd prefer to have.

Letting go of a relationship that we know is bad for us is difficult to do. Sometimes we stay in the relationship so long that we don't realize the damage we're causing to ourselves. We will grow and blossom into the beautiful butterfly, once we let go and learn to fly solo!

My addiction to Prince Charming lasted too long. I didn't want to leave him or our Castle because we were going to live "Happily Ever After" forever! Breaking up is hard to do. Staying apart is even harder! When you keep calling him, finding excuses to connect with him, you know you have an addiction. You have to release your grip in order to use both hands to help yourself out of the mess!

Drowning in the alligator filled waters of the moat surrounding the Castle is not how you want this "fairy tale" to end. Swim to shore, and begin anew. Start over with renewed determination to attract only that which is best for you. Day Dreams come true, so start day dreaming!

Journal, keep an "Illustrated Discovery Journal" and paste things you want to manifest into a spiral bound artist's notebook. See yourself succeeding, overcoming the obstacles and making that choice to be happy. See yourself creating your own "Happily Ever After". You can do it!

The Magic Wand of Friendship

With the touch of a Magic Wand, friendship can touch your life and make everything seem right with the world again. We need our girlfriends to confide in and to laugh with. They'll tell us the truth, if we're lucky, and they'll listen as we sob about the latest drama with Prince Charming. They are the cheerleaders in our lives.

Yesterday I was having coffee with a girlfriend and as we listened to each other I realized that her compassion and empathy for me, as mine for her, was the soothing balm that we all need to keep going. This journey we take is not meant to be a lonely one. We are meant to have Joy in our lives! A friend can bring the joy by being a listening ear and walking with us.

To know there is someone else who is going through something as similar to what I am brings a sense of validation, and also lets us know that we're not alone.

I'd spent too much time in the Castle, alone, writing this book. Not venturing out to explore, laugh and have fun, making things feel heavier and harder for me. A friendship is like a magic wand in that it's almost like "magic" that you feel so much better when you're with your friend doing something fun.

When was the last time you and a friend went out for fun? Make plans to take a class, go for a walk, take a drive, go to the salon, or meet at the movies.

There is the added bonus that you can hug your friend, if you'd like, and studies have shown that you need at least 4 hugs a day for maintenance, 8 hugs a day for growth. There are chemicals that are released when you hug and when you smile and laugh. You need these happy chemicals to help maintain good mental health. You especially need this if you're new to being on your own, without a companion.

You can use the "Day Dreams Come True" method to attract a friend into your life just the same way that you use it for anything else that you want. I marveled at how much my new friend and I had in common and how she was so much like me. It affirmed that my manifesting was, once again, working quite well, as she was the perfect addition to my life!

Using the Day Dreaming Method™ is good practice for manifesting the important people you want in your life. I find it to be such a kick to watch it unfold, before my very eyes, like magic.

Remember to make a visual journal by ripping photos out of magazines and pasting them into a notebook, write in the notebook what you specifically want to manifest, and then take time to close your eyes and visualize this manifestation coming true. There is a feeling you'll get when you are speaking about it, as you visualize, where you're in the present and past tense of the thing you want to manifest. When you feel that feeling, stay with it as long as you can and hold onto it, remember it and refer back to it as often as you can. Intentionally go to bed with that feeling on your mind and allow it to fill your senses. The more energy you put into the manifesting, the sooner that which you wish for will come true!

I've done this over and over in my life and continue to marvel at the results. Try it and watch great things manifest in your life, too!

Manifesting Support & Coaching

One of the best ways to keep your energetic frequency at a higher vibration is to surround yourself with people who are doing the same thing. That's why I've created several ways to support you along your journey.

Choose to participate in any of these communities:

The Manifesting Princess secret Facebook Group, is by invitation only. To join, go to my website, www.ManifestingPrincess.com and click on "Coaching". The monthly fee includes community membership, a twice monthly Question and Answer phone call, and a lot of support within the group. You won't want to miss out on this opportunity to be with people who are manifesting their inner Princess!

Private Coaching is available as well. We meet for 30 minutes, by phone, and I can help you achieve your manifesting goals. Contact me by going to www.ManifestingPrincess.com and click on "Coaching" to buy time and set up an appointment.

One thing I did, when I was first starting out, I started a "Law of Attraction" book club in my area and we read and discussed different books by different authors on the subject. It's fun, free and a great way to meet new people in your community, while raising your vibration! Request additional books directly from me by emailing me at info@ManifestingPrincess.com and I might even stop by, via internet, to chat with your group some time! Just let me know!

Also, do the Manifesting Assignments in the next chapter to keep yourself on track and your vibrational frequency as high as possible!

I wish you all the very best and please remember that I am here for you!

You can find me at my website at www.ManifestingPrincess.com, or on www.AprilClineRadio.com with the Manifesting Princess show.

You can also find me on Facebook.com/ManifestingPrincess or Twitter.com/PrincessofLOA. I'm always happy to help you out.

I spend most of my time with my group coaching community, so be sure to join and we can participate in more things there.

You are a beautiful light to the world. Step into your ruby slippers and become the Manifesting Princess you were always meant to be! You will be a shining example by living UP to the Reputation!

Be sure to be home by the "stroke of midnight" and Happy Manifesting!

april ♥

Manifesting Assignments

What would you do if you knew you couldn't fail? Tell me about yourself. Do you like yourself? Do you like your life? Do you think you're pretty? Are you proud of your accomplishments? Do you think you're someone special? Are you worth knowing?

This is where Vision Boards (see next chapter) can be so helpful. Tear out photos, words, etc., from magazines and paste them into a spiral bound artist's book – or even a simple school notebook that your kid isn't using anymore. Handwrite your dreams and desires on the pages. Fill them up and look at the "vision" as often as you possibly can, but especially before you go to bed.

When you go to bed, decide what you're going to dream about. I began doing this when I was a little girl. I used to have favorite stories to keep me occupied until I fell asleep. I still do it to this day.

Another thing I did was I found a great photo of a couple in love and put it as my screen saver on my computer. It has been there for about three years now. This instantly raises my vibration. Get a photo for your screen saver and daydream about the high vibrational energy you feel from that photo.

Dress immaculately. Your grooming should be worthy of a Princess! How can you manifest when you're a mess? Clean up, fix up and straighten up and you will *Live UP to the Reputation of the Manifesting Princess!*

Write down five things you're Grateful for, right now…. You'll be so grateful that you did!

Stand in front of a mirror and say the following: I love life and life loves me. (Louise Hay). Life Loves Me. Life Loves Me. (say it again) LIFE LOVES ME! Now take out your cell phone and text yourself – LIFE LOVES ME and post it on your Facebook wall, tweet it and go back to the mirror and write it in lipstick across the mirror.

Serving others is also an excellent way to raise your vibration and also give back. It tells the Universe that you're grateful, that you feel the abundance in your life so much that you're willing to take the time to spend time with others who need someone to visit with them, or to help them in some way.

Lie down in a comfortable position, close your eyes and start to visualize your dream. Imagine what it would feel like to be there. What are some of the sights, sounds and smells? What does it feel like? What are you wearing?

What are you doing? Imagine that you are in that dream doing exactly what you've dreamed of doing. Now hold that feeling and just stay in that day dream feeling for as long as you can. That is the feeling that will ATTRACT the dream to you like a MAGNET!

Now it's your turn. What is your heart's desire? What dream are you wishing? Maybe you haven't even told yourself because it seemed silly or unrealistic. It's really not! You can have anything you dream of if you want it badly enough!

Create a Vision Board

They say a picture is worth a thousand words! I think it's worth millions of dollars! Creating a Vision Board can literally bring you millions, so why not create the Vision Board with everything you're dreaming about?

I'm a visual person and so it's very important to me to be able to see what my goals are and what I want to manifest.

It's also nice to have visuals that will raise my vibrational frequency just by looking at them. A beautiful picture can elevate your energy very quickly and keep you in that higher frequency that you need in order to "stay attractive" to the other energetic flow of the same frequency.

You can create your Vision Board on paper, or in a notebook, or there are even software programs to create them. I even have a fancy spiral bound artist's notebook that I have pasted magazine photos and words into. I highlighted it with markers and wrote on it and even bedazzled it for that BLING effect! But I can honestly say that it is too much work and I end up procrastinating!

To make things easier, I just open up a blank Word document and start inserting photos and sayings that I have found on Facebook (I don't know who they belong to, so I can't give credit; I should be more diligent about that), and then I save the document, or print it out and hang it up some place where I will see it often.

I have a WALL in my bedroom where I have placed all of my Vision Board documents! It's so inspirational and comes in real handy when I am doing down into the dungeon and want to lift myself UP very quickly!

So, you can do whatever you want. Use the spiral bound artist's notebook, a school notebook, blank paper, or go and buy fancy software, or just open your computer and open up a blank Word document page. I set mine to "landscape" and then I start adding photos that I have saved on my hard drive especially for the Vision Board.

It's so much fun, and a great way to do some active Day Dreaming, so indulge as often as you can!

I'm including a few pages for you to look at here in this book as inspiration. You could print them out and hand-write on them your different comments or goals, or type words on labels and then just tape them on the printed page. It's up to you. Just be sure you're having fun, dreaming and planning your manifestations! Go for it my Manifesting Princess!!

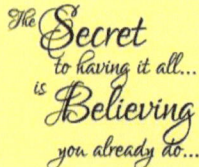

"THE WOMAN WHO FOLLOWS THE CROWD WILL USUALLY GO NO FURTHER THAN THE CROWD. THE WOMAN WHO WALKS ALONE IS LIKELY TO FIND HERSELF IN PLACES NO ONE HAS EVER BEEN BEFORE."
-ALBERT EINSTEIN

  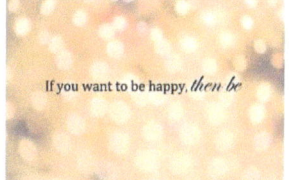

Quotes by April Cline

(Unless otherwise indicated)

When I thought better of myself, and what I deserved, what I should and shouldn't live with (or without), when I stood my ground, when I spoke my truth, I found out that I was not alone, that I was loved, that I was liked, and I received greater respect.

She is a Princess at making her dreams into a reality and knows that everything she thinks and does today will be what she reaps tomorrow.

If you've never focused on yourself before, then you're going to have a bit of a bumpy ride. You have to know yourself and who you are in order to even know what to dream about, wish for, and manifest.

What you put in front of the mirror is a direct reflection, literally, of how you feel about yourself.

Please don't wait until you've had a hurricane in order to feel the wind!

A Dream is a Wish Your Heart Makes
~ **Cinderella**

Be happy and continue moving forward as you light the world.

Walk your talk. Rise to the occasion and continue on your journey to Live Up to the Reputation of being a Manifesting Princess!

Energetically your vibrational frequency is so attractive that you will be sought after by many, simply because they want to know what your "secret" is. And the best part is that you can tell them, if they're ready to listen!

You are enough.

There is a certain peace that comes from ending the struggle, and going with the flow – the energetic flow of life and the Universal Law of Attraction.

It is a choice to be happy. What will you choose?

For me, it has been life changing because I feel myself sending out wondrous waves of energy that will draw him to me, eventually, when I'm ready.

I create my reality – it's really true!

The silence was deafening and defining!

The same is true about lack. If you focus on the loss and the things wrong in your life, what you're lacking – watch how quickly you have more lack.

Gratitude changes everything and raises your vibrational energy exponentially!

> Receive the world for which it is, not what it's not.
> ~ **Unknown**

> No matter how your heart is grieving, if you keep on believing, the dreams that you wish, will come true!
> ~ **Cinderella**

LIFE LOVES ME.
~ **Louise Hay**

There are No Victims, only Volunteers!

You can't afford the luxury of a negative thought.

It's okay to lose your way, but it's not okay to stay there.

Stand for something or you'll fall for anything.

We teach people how to treat us.
~ **Dr. Phil**

What would you do if you knew you couldn't fail?

"Your thoughts are powerful, attractive magnets – attracting one to another. Thoughts attract to themselves, and you attract thoughts to you by giving your attention to them. Those who speak most of prosperity have it, and those who speak most of sickness or poverty have it. It is Law. It can be no other way."
~ **Abraham-Hicks**

"By intending – as you are moving into a segment of relationships – to focus upon your points of harmony; to give your great attention, not to what you are disagreeing about, but to the things you agree upon…that is the resolution in all relationships. For when you focus on what you do not like, by the Law of Attraction, you solicit more of what you do not want."

~ Abraham-Hicks

"I can create Castles as easily as buttons! When you understand the Laws, then you understand that it is not more difficult to create a castle than it is a button. They are equal. It is not more difficult to create $10 million than $100,000. It is the same application of the same Law to two different intentions."

~ Abraham-Hicks

If you want tomorrow to be happy, then be happy today!

Quotes & Stories from Friends

Julie Turner from Australia writes:

My favourite LOA quote is from Hemal: "Say to self: 'Despite what I have been through, I am going to go through the best period of my life and it will be phenomenal.' " ~ *Hemal Radia*

I needed money to fly my family to Darwin, Australia for my university graduation ceremony. At this time I only had 78 cents in the bank. I knew I would manifest this money using the LOA. On the 5th September 2011, I asked the Universe for $6,000 by <u>end of September</u> but the money manifested itself within two days. Unexpected monies were deposited into my bank account on 6th and 7th September 2011. All because I asked the Universe, let it go, visualised and the $$ turned up! (I sent Hemal my bank statement as proof). This is twice this year that I have asked for $6,000 and the first time it manifested within 5 days and this time it manifested within 2 days.

April, just to share with you, what keeps me constantly in the flow is I try to attract happiness each day before the sun sets. Whatever I ask the Universe for, it usually manifest before the sun set each and every single day, whether it may be a fresh flower from someone, or asking the universe for someone to take me to the movies (of my choice) or shout me dinner (of my choice). But by attracting happiness into my life daily, it is helping me stay in the flow and (I believe - my opinion here) I believes it speeeeeds things up for me to manifest the things I want. Therefore I attract happiness first to be happy and be aligned with the vibrational energies to manifest whatever I want. Since I've been constantly attracting happiness first (you know the story how I lost my three children, so through my pain and through my grief, <u>I HAVE TO MAKE MYSELF HAPPY</u> by attracting happiness) and since I been constant attracting happiness first, I am amazed at the sppeeeeed of my manifestations! Maybe this is the key to the speed of manifestations? Mumuck and thank you April.

Julie Turner, Australia

Hema Parmar from United Kingdom writes:

I left my job as a Sales Manager in a fashion company last year, and I've been living back with my parents. Which was hard for me, but it was the best decision ever.

I have chilled out and I am having an amazing time with my parents.

Anyway, I want to start working, but not in the same kind of job I was doing, the thought of that job really has got me stress out.

I have always wanted to run/open up a Lifestyle Boutique having home-ware art/ crafts from around the world, but I've never had the guts or the financial means, however I believed I would one day.

I was searching some blogs which I found very interesting - a lifestyle boutique in Portland, USA. They were actually advertising for a role something similar to what I wanted, but I did not want to move there. So, I copied the job spec, and made it my own, *like I had been accepted for the job.*

It was just so thrilling to write the job spec, I felt so amazing; I put it up on my vision board.

Now I felt I was going to get a job like it, but I kept asking myself HOW.

Being on the manifesting group calls has been amazing, as Hemal really helped in me focusing on my goals and learning how to keep my vibrations raised. One of the exercises Hemal gave me was to free write, anything and everything I felt I wrote down.... I soon felt elevated and happy, I also wrote a future timeline where I would get a job end September, however that really frightened me as it felt too soon, as we were in July.

A few times I felt really, really down, as friends around me were getting jobs and I was out of work for a year, not that I had been looking but it just made me feel 'crap'. By the end of August I read a post by you, April, on the group wall, it was a Wed eve... it was about Letting Go and its amazing what you achieve.... oh boy, I just don't know what happened, but I felt so relieved and light (So THANK YOU FOR YOUR POST THAT DAY!).

The next day, I got a call from a cousin who lives in Africa, she rang me up and said, "Fancy coming to Africa and setting up a lifestyle boutique with me?" She will finance me, and I get to do stuff I LOVE to do. I mean come on, that is super cool and so LOA!!!

Also, on the group, we played the prosperity game, where you have £100 and you double it each day and write all the wonderful things you would like to spend with it.

Well, when I got to a few millions, I wanted to open up a few lifestyle boutiques across the world and help cottage industries local artists.

What do you know, once I'm up and running the lifestyle boutique in Africa, we will be supporting local artist and cottage industries.

Hema Parmar, UK

Chessie Roberts from USA writes:

I am a 61 year old woman who, 11 years ago, was dependent on schedule 2 narcotics and a wheelchair until I decided to stop being ill. As I got better, my chiropractor asked me what I was doing to get better so quickly and that I should tell people.

Using the tenets of the Law of Attraction to create healing within both my body and my mind I was healing. As I continued to change on the inside and it showed so dramatically on the outside, I began to feel that he was right and, again using the Law of Attraction to assist me, I created and manifested a program that is now called Evolution of Self *(http://mysite.verizon.net/vze15r6ar/eos/)*; Journey into Body, Mind, Spirit Balance to continue the healthy shift and balance shift within myself.

I was then able to share it with others in a way to spread a positive, healthy, forward moving mind set. The program has grown into a viable set of classes that provide training in cohesive steps that anyone who is really serious about helping themselves to create this mindset can easily incorporate into their daily lives. As I have continued to use the Law of Attraction along with some Eastern philosophies, EoS also has grown to include (*with information that I received from my Guidance and The*

Ascended Masters) to help others entrain with the planet in preparation for the shift that is building.

Chessie Roberts, Virginia USA

This story takes place long before I became aware of the" Law of Attraction" which, to me, makes it even more awesome because it happened naturally. I was living in a very small apartment with my two children & my mom and I was working for next to nothing at a laundromat. I decided one day that we needed a bigger space to fit us comfortably and prayed/intended to have it come my way. Within one (1) week a friend of mine came to me and said she was moving. She asked me if I wanted to take over her home. It was a huge 2 story / 3.5 bedrooms / 2 baths home and I wanted it. So I spoke to the landlord and he let me repaint the whole house to pay for deposit. I was so excited about how fast this house came into our lives that I didn't even realize, until after we were moved in, that I didn't make enough money at my current job to support the new bills. So I made a new prayer/intention for a better job that would provide more income and proceeded to put in my two weeks' notice. One (1) week later I walked into my landlord's business to pay rent and he asked me if I knew how to be a secretary. I said yes, even though I had never done this type of work before, knowing I could learn quickly. He told me to put in my two weeks' notice at my other job and I told him, "Yeah, I did that a week ago."

That was almost 8 years ago and we are still in the same house and I still have the same job, several raises later. We are all comfortable and doing well because I was not afraid to step out and have a little faith

Hope my story suits your desires for your book. I will keep my eye out for a notice as to whether or not it has been chosen. Thank you for providing me with an opportunity to share one of "many" LOA stories I have experienced in my life.

Dusty Caraway, USA

We are STRONGER when together...Life throws its blows on our faces, our victory lies in taking those blows as challenges and facing them with a smile...Nothing stays the same forever, neither good times nor bad ones. All we have to do is stay in there...strong and firm in the face of storms.

~ Sherry Shereen

Always try to make the best of everything and make the best of what you got, rather than feeling inferior to others' achievements. Excel in yourself and in your own capabilities.

~ Sherry Shereen

God tests our patience, our strength by putting us in situations Just to see how strong we are.

~ Sherry Shereen

It's sad how we all seem so cheerful, bubbly and happy.... but carry so much sadness inside our hearts.

~ Sherry Shereen

The dreams we dream while awake are the dreams that can be actually accomplished.

~ Sherry Shereen

Your heart beats rhythms to your soul's rhymes;
Look into your soul for your own melodies divine.
~ Sherry Shereen

You can create your own melodies. Just look into your soul for rhymes and rhythms.
~ Sherry Shereen

Imagine, dream, visualize and believe in your dreams. Life is full of endless possibilities; the doors are all open to opportunities, success, prosperity, health, love and happiness. It's all out there for you to go and make it all yours...Dream it, believe it, and achieve it.
~ Sherry Shereen

Floating endlessly on the clouds of fancy~~Drowned forever into the depths of Passion.
~ Sherry Shereen

Feelings~~feelings~~feelings~~only feelings~~~Feelings of being LOVED~~ feelings of friendship~~feelings of BEing~~feelings of love!! True, 'Best things in life are feelings not things.'

~ Sherry Shereen

The reality won't change...better change yourself.

~ Sherry Shereen

Healthy Thoughts" & " Positive Approaches" bring in "Positive & Healthy Results.

~ Sherry Shereen

If You Begin....Infinite Follows.

~ Joseph Smith, Jr.

Don't chase perfect moments. Simply, open the door and invite them in.

~ Debbie Bhangoo

Recommended

For information about the International Association of Law of Attraction Professionals, founded by Katherine CHE, please visit the website at www.iaLOAp.org .

About April Cline

April Cline is the mother of three sons and two darling daughters-in-law. She is an Author, Speaker, Law of Attraction certified Life Coach and Host of The April Cline Radio Show. She enjoys French impressionist paintings, making perfume, singing, and photography. She loves giving intimate dinner parties, and writing inspiring books. She lives in an enchanted cottage with her cat, Monet, in West Virginia.

You are

Cordially Invited to

Live Your Life

Happily Ever After!

With Love,

April Cline

www.ManifestingPrincess.com

www.ingramcontent.com/pod-product-compliance
Lightning Source LLC
Chambersburg PA
CBHW042308150426
43198CB00001B/10